Woman to Women

By
Rebecca Bryant Hervey

From a Series of
God-Inspired Letters
Written and Mailed Especially
to Women.

ChinaberryTree
Publishing

Woman to Women

by Rebecca Bryant Hervey

Scripture quotations are from:
The Holy Bible, New International Version (NIV)
Copyright 1986 by Holman Bible Publishers

The Holy Bible, King James Version (KJV)
Franklin Electronic Bible

CHINABERRY TREE PUBLISHING
64 Sam Thomas Rd. # 7
Texarkana, Texas 75501

Table of Contents

"Begin"

Good Morning!

As I was sitting at the table this morning with my usual cup of coffee and the crossword puzzle in the newspaper... my mode of waking up my brain.... I felt the Lord's Presence come over me in a wonderful way. Immediately I stopped what I was doing and worshipped Him. Then I seemed to hear Him say that I should turn off the lights, go and get my journal, which is a notebook I try to write in daily; so I did that, though wondering how I was going to write in the journal in the semi-darkness. Opened the journal and waited for the Lord to tell me something. After a few minutes I heard Him say, "Begin to write". More waiting, to see what else He had to tell me. Instead of hearing Him say anything else, I began to remember that during the past several weeks I've felt that He wanted me to write to women and remind them of scriptures that reveal the joys of being a woman, and also of the responsibilities of a woman. So I wrote this message in my journal, "Begin to write", so that in the busy-ness of my life I will be reminded of what the Lord has given me to do.... which is to write the things He directs me to write.

That isn't hard to do, for me! I love to write letters! And I love to share the things the Lord has shown me in His marvelous Word that are being overlooked in this age of working wives and mothers. Many times those women who stay at home and keep house and raise their children feel that there's nothing "glorious" for them to do. Many of them get into the habit of entertaining themselves with television until the man of the house comes home for supper in the evening. The woman who is sometimes called a "non-working" wife or mother may feel like a clock with no battery or electricity! Non-working! Well, not according to the Word of God!! We need to study, not just read casually, the description of a virtuous, or noble, woman according to Him who created us! It's exciting to turn to Proverbs 31, beginning with verse 10, and see what a woman can do!! This woman isn't just sitting around all day waiting to be made valid or needed when her husband comes home! The woman in verse 11 has her husband's full confidence. Look how she works! She does something worthwhile with her hands. She keeps her household in order. What? She even works in Real Estate? :) This little figure :) is a computer smile, in case anyone wonders. A frown would be :(

The virtuous woman sets about her work vigorously; her arms are strong for her tasks. Look at v. 20. "She opens her arms to the poor and extends her hands to the needy." It reminds me of my own precious mother, who after raising nine children, suffered several years with a heart condition that was at that time inoperable and untreatable. She died when I, her youngest, was eighteen years of age.... but her lessons to me continue to live on in fond memories. She and my father never had much money, yet they had plenty and to share. Why? Because they worked diligently with what they had. Even with her heart giving her trouble, Mama tended a garden, raised chickens, milked a cow, helped my dad raise a few hogs. With these resources and their constant effort, my parents found great joy in being able to give of whatever they had, which was not much. Eggs, fresh from the henhouse. A gallon of cold, fresh milk. Sweet country butter, buttermilk, a pint of fresh cream to go with the peaches they'd picked. Armloads of fresh vegetables, home-canned vegetables, even ham or bacon or sausage, and Mama's specialty, fresh Applesauce-banana cake. The day she died, I'm told, was one of her most joyful days. People drove from town to their little ten-acre farm just to buy fresh eggs, and went away with armloads of whatever was ripe from the garden, having been joyfully led on a tour of the farm by my mother, and treated to a choice blossom from her beloved rosebushes. She wore herself out being hospitable, but it gave her the greatest joy. That night she experienced the heart attack that carried her from this world into the arms of Jesus. It was agony for me to lose her. Horrible agony! ...but now that I'm older and know Him better, I can see that my loss was not only heaven's gain, but Mama's gain. I can't imagine her resting on a fluffy cloud in heaven and doing nothing. She must be singing, as she always sang or whistled as she worked on earth during her 54 years here. If there are gardens, I know hers is full of roses she lovingly tends so that she can pass them around for all to enjoy. I know the choicest of her roses go to her beloved Lord and Savior, about whom she loved to sing. We, her children, call her blessed, and a blessing! Many women do noble things, but she surpassed them all. Charm is deceptive, and beauty is fleeting; but a woman who fears the Lord is to be praised. Give her the reward she has earned, and let her works bring her praise at the city gate. (from Prov. 31)

She and our father taught us from the Bible through living it before us. Even though my father didn't really know the joy of salvation until just before his death at age 91, he knew some scriptures, and quoted them to us as we grew. He must have had these in mind : From Proverbs 22, 'A prudent man sees danger and takes refuge, but the simple keep going and suffer for it." "Humility and fear of the Lord bring wealth and honor and life." "In the paths of the wicked lie thorns and snares, but he who guards his soul stays far from them." and the most oft-quoted... "Train a child in the way he should go, and when he is old he will not turn from it." There's also verse 9, "a generous man will himself be blessed, for he shares his food with the poor." We all need to find instruction and wisdom for life in this wonderful guidebook God has given us! In future letters I have thoughts from the Scriptures about raising children, and how to teach them, even as toddlers, to reverence the Lord so that their lives will be prosperous in every way. There are wonderful guidelines in God's Word for husbands and wives, for being a wise and effective individual no matter what your position in life... pleasing unto Him who created us not for our own pleasure but as a gift and inheritance for His Son Jesus. Guidelines that bring that elusive thing called JOY or PEACE OF MIND that the world searches for in vain without Him. I love you, and pray that you have found some sort of blessing from this letter. :)

In His Sweet Love,
Becky Hervey

"Fruitcake"

Hi!

Maybe not everyone enjoys this cool, drizzly weather, but I really, really do! I love the Fall season, when the trees are putting on their holiday dresses and then decorating the earth with their beauty, and the nip in the air reminds us it's Thanksgiving time...

I can serve my family turkey and dressing any time, and we love it all through the year. Don't even have to cook it if I don't want to; it's available at Bryce's Cafeteria the year 'round, but the one scrumptious delicacy you can't locate any time except this glorious season is..... fruitcake! I know, I'm one of the few genuine fruitcake lovers. And it really is hard to find a 'genuine' fruitcake...(unless you think I'm one! :) Those no-bake ones are probably what makes people hate fruitcake, y'know? Marsh-mallows and gumdrops? Gimme a break! I've gotta have the REAL THING or nothing. So I find the genuine articles and bake my own luscious fruitcake. So what if I have to eat it all myself? I hide it away and munch , secretly... and few there be that find it!   No, I'm not selfish with it, I just don't know that many people who will even taste it. They wrinkle up their noses and say, "Fruitcake? Yuuuuuck!"

It reminds me of entering the Kingdom of God. "Few there be that find it", and I was one of those for about half of my life who wrinkled up my nose and self-righteously refused to allow God to make me a 'genuine article'. I'd seen so much fakery that I perceived anyone who spoke freely about Jesus as Friend and Lord to be a flake or fanatic. I shuddered at the thought of it... just like the folks I know who don't like fruitcake! No... I'm not trying to sell fruitcake, and the Kingdom of God is free for the taking. It's a realm above the natural, and it isn't entered into casually. It has to be entered with one's whole heart, ... GENUINELY. It's like taking the "Nestea plunge", as Reed says... you may remember the TV ad where a person stands at the edge of a swimming pool and falls backward fearlessly into the cooling, refreshing water. Care, worry, heat and everything else is left behind, and he or she is entirely submersed in that cool, clear water. Well... "If he stays underwater too long he'll die!" There you go! Jesus told His disciples that they were IN the world, but not OF the world. Paul the Apostle wrote several times about DYING to the worldly realm as we knew it and LIVING a supernatural life, didn't he?

You're probably familiar with James 2:19 saying that even DEMONS believe there is only one God, and they TREMBLE, but that is not a SAVING kind of belief. They had turned their backs on God, even knowing who God is. In other words, they did not have FAITH in Him. They didn't commit their lives to Him, but followed the tempter instead. They chose a realm where He is not Lord.... Absolute Ruler.... Counselor... not even Friend.

Now, my letter is becoming "preachy", probably. But there's something valuable to take notice of here. Concerning we who believe and profess that Jesus is Lord, we can't just nod and say, "Well, yes, I believe". True believing is far, far more than attending church at the appropriate times, wearing T-shirts or jewelry proclaiming His Lordship, carrying a Bible or even **...(tremble-tremble-tremble—)** the **"T" word,"TITHING." :)** MORE than all these. Maybe I'm stepping on some toes,... Well, should I apologize? Forgive me if I'm meddling, but it just seems awfully important to me that we recognize the difference. To me it's the difference between being the Bride of Christ, and being the friends who'll be left behind like the five foolish virgins in Matthew 25. Personally, it's worth my life and everything to be in that Wedding Party, and I want the wedding party to include all those I love.

Lest there be any misunderstanding with what I said about tithing... I'm all for it. Can't live without it. I've just heard too many people who are struggling saying, "We just can't afford to tithe". And I say, "What!? You can't afford to stop robbing God? **What's wrong with this picture?" :(:)** Personally, we can't afford NOT to tithe, and as for giving... Whew! It is absolutely true about it being given back to us, pressed down, shaken together and running over! Our life is a joyful example of His faithfulness and goodness! I could tell you about it sometime, but few would believe it. It's too fantastic!

Going to close now and spend some time with the family. We're expecting a great-grandchild any time now... and other things are in the works that God has so swiftly put in order. He is so unspeakably wonderful! Our new mailing address may change, but only slightly. We'll be moving to the apartment upstairs. Gabriel and Amy (our grandson and granddaughter-in-law) will likely be getting new house-mates that God is bringing into our home, and they'll occupy the half of the apartment we were sharing. It's going to be a Christmas season to remember! Maybe in one of my letters I'll tell you about the program the Lord gave us that I dubbed "Honest Elbow Grease" to help sincere people learn to help themselves and grow in the Lord... God is sufficient.. It's HIS program, and if He isn't in it we can't do it, nor would we choose to! :) Have a Happy and Blessed Thanksgiving!

In His Sweet Love, **Becky Hervey**

"Purpose"

Well, Hello again!

I haven't finished my last mail-out yet, but the Lord has me awake here at 1 a.m. Instead of sleeping I found myself praying in the Spirit and thinking of things that are on my heart. Women everywhere need encouragement to be or to become what God created us to be, don't you think? Sorry to say, religious ideas gone sour have made folks think that a woman's place is strictly in the home. Me? I'm glad that's where the Lord wants me right now. The workplace and college served to train and educate me but it was very frustrating to this homebody. :) Yes, Proverbs 31 speaks of a woman working in her home, and not neglecting her family, etc... but some women are obviously ordained for other positions as well.

Consider Deborah, in Judges 4:4. She was a wife, but also a prophetess, and she judged Israel. Not only women came to her for advice, but men also. In verse 7 a man named Sisera is mentioned. Deborah prophesied to a man named Barak that Israel's enemy Sisera would be delivered into the hand of the Israelites. She even went with Barak to carry out God's command. Hey.. this woman had a husband at home named Lapidoth. Why didn't God tell Lapidoth to go with Barak? I guess it's because He chooses whom he wants to choose and sends whom He wants to send. What? Who captured and killed Sisera? Not Barak. Not Deborah, but another woman. God Himself caused Sisera to be afraid and to run and hide even though he had nine thousand chariots of warriors. And even though Barak had ten thousand men fighting with him, Sisera.. it is written... fled on foot to the tent of the wife of a man named Heber, whose named was Jael. It's very interesting to read. This woman Jael was used of God. She didn't fight him like a man. She waited until he was asleep and drove a tent spike through his head with a hammer! All this was for the purpose of bringing peace to Israel at that time.

Purpose! God has a PURPOSE for each and every one of us, male, female, married, unmarried... and He sets into our hearts a desire to know and find that purpose. As for myself, I knew even as a small child that God had created me to draw pictures and to sing. It was only later that the gift of writing developed and was encouraged by English teachers in school. I loved to make things! Whatever was at hand could turn out to be something useful or pretty. My Grandma often wore a silk dress that had tiny polka dots very similar to the feathers of the guinea fowl that roamed our farmyard. I wanted to turn those beautiful feathers into something to keep, but Mama said they were "nasty" and forbade me to pick them up. Mama wasn't cruel, she just didn't think the way I did.

God's purpose for my life is still unfolding. He's using the experiences of my lifetime to enable me to encourage others. Well, I have a really interesting background! Anyone need some encouragement? I've been a high-school dropout, a teen bride and mother. I've been divorced...more than once! Got my GED certificate at age 35 and went to college that summer. Worked as a nurse aide while trying to keep my brood of kids together in some semblance of family. Far from perfect am I, but still, God has a purpose for me. In 1971 I stopped fighting God over the subject of "speaking in tongues", and allowed Him to bless me immeasurably with that wonderful outpouring known as the Baptism in the Holy Spirit. In that moment He set me free from 21 years of chronic bronchitis and hay fever, released me from the fear of singing to a crowd of people, where previously I feared speaking to even five or six strangers.

Since that day He has given me songs to sing, stories to write, and sometimes I have felt so frustrated with my overflowing creativity that I cried out, "God! I repent of this creative urge in me. Deliver me from it so I can serve You!" And all He said in reply was, "I AM the CREATOR, I HAVE PUT THIS URGE IN YOU TO CREATE. DO IT!" So I got out of bed at four in the morning, started a bowl of yeast bread dough to rise, and made a papier mache cat. The bread was soon consumed by anyone who came by and smelled it baking. The papier mache cat has sat for about 18 years atop my daughter Cindi's kitchen cupboards, looking down at her growing brood of five sons and one daughter. It isn't what one would call pretty, but it's kind of a conversation piece. If they like it that's all that matters to me. Her walls are decorated with my paintings, no matter how imperfect. Likewise my other children's homes. The works of art say to them that Mom loves. Loves to make, loves to give, loves them!

In 1984, at the age of 49, I found myself in a crisis shelter for women and children. Before long I had a night job at that very place and enrolled once more in college for 2 1/2 years, and just kept plugging away at trying to believe God in spite of all my perilous

11

adventures and keep following Him. He's faithful! I couldn't get any more tuition so I dropped the college studies, but the Lord gave me a job with a salary of $500. a week. That was LOTS of money for me, but after 1 and 1/2 years the Lord commanded me to get back to Texarkana. I mean, commanded! I'm so glad I obeyed! He gave me another job, equally prosperous, and a friend who became my husband the following year. We are deliriously happy... most of the time. :) Sometimes we're just delirious!

We've been married for six fantastic years now, and life gets better and better as we learn to lay down what we considered "our" lives and let Him live through us. Desires and ambitions have changed, but the gifts He put into us and the drive to accomplish certain things have been polished and made stronger with time. Who would ever think that the gift of singing and writing gospel songs would still be usable now that I'm 63 years old? But we're almost finished with the album on a CD. Don't know what we'll call it yet. Okay, end of page 3. This is enough for now. I dare you to turn loose and trust God to make of you what He designed and ordained you to be!

He is more than faithful... it's also His desire for your desires to be met! I love you, and hey... it's okay to drop me a line if you want to.

Have a happy day, in Jesus' sweet love,
Becky

"Cradle"

Praise to the Lord!

Before I can finish one mail-out, the Lord wakes me up with another letter, and from the first mailing list of 20 women, we're now nearing 100. I LOVE the Lord's ways. Although I was up until 12:30 last night printing out the last additions to letter #3, He woke me gently at 5:30 this morning....and although I tried to go back to sleep; at 6 a.m. I heard Him say..."The hand that rocks the cradle...." and the immensity of what that means finally came home to me!

I've heard that phrase all my life, and I think it comes from a poem, but that's all I remember..."The hand that rocks the cradle is the hand that rules the world." The thought immediately hit me about the condition the world is in today, and how, if more mothers had prayed for their babies as they rocked that cradle... and if they had raised those children with Godly principles so that when they are old they would not depart from them... what a different world this would be! Now... I'm not suggesting that we all get the mullygrubs about what we didn't do, but that we see the light about what we can teach and proclaim! A mother who loves her children, gives them affection, direction and discipline, will reap what she sows, and her children will affect the condition of the world for good!

In the same way, a mother who just lets her children "happen"... and allows them to form their own set of rules and live in disobedience; a mother who actually obeys her children rather than making it the other way around... that mother will be raising a child who is not only miserable but makes those around him or her miserable...which will also affect the condition of the world, tragically! I've seen it at close hand, in a very dear relative who refused to teach her young children about Jesus or read the Bible to them. She raised a houseful of offspring with no sense of direction about their lives; following their own feelings and opinions, who are now adults in their forties and fifties and follow after strange gods, living according to the world's loose standards. She's gone now, but left behind some very bitter and unhappy people whose cradles were not rocked with a hand that reached out to God in their behalf. Don't get me wrong, she was a delightful person in many ways. Her children were not 'bad' kids. They were adventurous, creative, inquisitive. Family gatherings at her house were a highlight of the entire clan who lived anywhere near her... but she herself, though jolly and personable on the outside, was a woman with a heart full of bitterness and unforgiveness, which transferred to her children. Two of them died in their youth, with illicit drugs in the picture. Those who are living do not know the Lord nor do they want to in the truest sense of the word. Like a bunch of porcupines, they can't be touched deeply, unless the Lord in His sovereignty chooses to draw them to Himself, which I've always prayed that He would.

This is not to say that I was a perfect mother, oh, no! Plunged into motherhood at the tender age of 17, I'm so glad my own mother was there to help and guide me. And I had a pastor who looked askance at what we term "baby dedications" and instead suggested that parents dedicate **themselves** to raising a Godly and healthy, and well-disciplined child. Our church had no need for a nursery for children three and over; those children learned reverence for the house of the Lord quite early in life. Sitting obediently beside their parents. they learned to sing hymns and to know that the Bible was a holy book. Sure, they'd soon fall asleep during the sermons... as did some of the adults...:) but they knew that Jesus loved them and that the church was not a play-place. If they didn't learn it right off, a trip outside for firm discipline soon corrected that problem.

It was through my own poor judgment and lack of self-discipline as a mother that my innocent children endured the tragedy of divorce and other, far worse terrors; such as physical, mental and sexual abuse by a pseudo-repentant stepfather. Thirty years later they continue to suffer from the memories of those days... 13 years during which I didn't serve the Lord as I should have in order to keep peace with an unbelieving, unfaithful, ill-tempered husband, and my prayers fell unheard from the ceiling. For four years preceding that neither I nor my young mate took our marriage seriously and it soon ended in divorce. Each of us was caught up in a fantasy about someone we knew in high school who rocked our world! To be truthful, I did not give up that fantasy until I was 35 years old.. and even then it haunted me.

Psychologists today will advocate that fantasies are harmless and may even enhance a marriage. Hogwash! No woman or man should entertain fantasies about another person while relating to their own mate!

Whatever we contemplate in our heart is known to God, and I frankly admit that in my heart I lived in adultery although never physically being unfaithful in marriage! Was I 'rocking the cradle' with a righteous hand? No way! I thank God for His mercy to my children in bringing them through some terrible times in spite of my immaturity and ignorance!. But I did teach my children about Jesus. I either sent them or took them to Sunday School and made them know that the Lord's house was to be reverenced. They all know that Jesus is the King of Kings and Lord of Lords, whether they fully serve and adore Him or not at this moment. They will. God's Word says they will, and I stand on it with firm assurance. After all, I bowed...

At some point in my life, Jesus Christ of Nazareth, and not my own fleshly desires, became my true ruler... which I am quite sure was my mother's prayer for me. Mama might have prayed harder for me than for the rest of her children, because I was such a noodlehead! Caught up in fantasies and my own sense of excitement, I darted in one direction after another, only to be disappointed. Her voice still rings in my memory.."Rebecca, Rebecca, Rebecca! When will you ever learn?" Well, Mama... I've learned. It took lumps and bumps and bruises, but I've learned to let Jesus be absolute ruler and Lord of my life... even to getting out of bed early in the morning, which I'm sure she NEVER thought I'd do! :) I am so thankful to the Lord that HE has joined me in marriage with a man of God so we can serve Him with our lives, and amend some of the wrongs we've both done before becoming obedient to Him. Life in total obedience to the Lord is anything but dull! Each day is fuller and more exciting. By the time this letter reaches you, our Honest Elbow Grease program will likely be housing two more men who want desperately to let God take over and make of their lives what He designed them to be. His love is unfathomable, and because of His Sweet Love, I love you.

Becky Hervey

"Christmas"

Happy Holidays to you and yours!

This year it's seemed like Christmas to me for the past two months! Not just the fruitcake, although I did eat the WHOLE THING!....(it took two weeks). God's Spirit is so near, and so strong in our lives! Gabe finished his GED with flying colors, in case I forgot to mention that, and he's just becoming a man so rapidly it leaves us with our jaws hanging open! :) This week he's in Pensacola Florida attending the Brownsville Revival while also checking out a Bible School down there. Amy and little Asa are with us, and they're doing great! Asa is 11 lbs now at just about 2 weeks of age. His first medical checkup was very good.

I have so many things I want to say... and the Lord just keeps feeding things into my mind like you'd program a computer... but I'm going to share with you at this wonderful season something I wrote quite some time ago. It was published in a Pueblo, Colorado newspaper as the first prize winner in a contest about "My Most Memorable Christmas." For my $25. gift certificate at Safeway, instead of buying a Christmas turkey I bought a huge, gorgeous hanging fern, which I promptly and quite effectively killed! Never, never stick Plantstick fertilizer down into a pot of thickly grown fern! But on to my story.

If I'm going to keep this from being four pages I'd better get to the story itself. Hope you enjoy it!

LITTLE GIRLS' DREAMS REALLY CAN COME TRUE

It was the same Christmas season that I got a spanking for taking my sister's dare to run across the snowy yard in my bare feet. I'd always been a very sickly child, but that year I was fine. It had snowed just enough to give us a White Christmas in Idabel, Oklahoma... and Edna and I were enjoying it to the hilt. She was almost 10. I was 6 and a half. The year was 1941. She'd said that I was too much of a baby to take off my boots and run across the yard barefooted.

Making her promise not to tell on me, I zipped across the snowy yard in my bare feet just as Mama stepped out the front door to call us to breakfast. I got the spanking for risking my delicate health. Edna got her satisfaction. She'd already decided that I was too big to believe in Santa Claus, so she informed me in wicked big-sister whispers that it was really Mama and Daddy who filled our stockings, and not only that but we were so poor I would definitely NOT get the big baby doll in the pink silk dress I'd been hoping and praying for. I was sure she was wrong... but we'd see.

Christmas Eve night I cried myself to sleep after staying awake long enough to observe my parents in the living room, filling our long cotton stockings with the customary goodies of Christmastime. And I saw there was no big baby doll in a pink dress... only a very small rubber doll that drank from a bottle and wet its diaper, same as the year before. But finally sleeping, I dreamed.

In my dream, Santa Claus had not been able to come down the chimney because of hot coals from the fire in the fireplace, so he had placed on Mama's trunk in the garage.. wrapped in tissue paper, my heart's delight... a beautiful big baby doll that filled both my arms! Her shiny blue eyes opened and closed. Her dark painted hair was molded into a curl on top of her head; and her dress.... Oh! I could actually FEEL the silk of it!

I awoke in the still of dawn just from the excitement of feeling that silk dress between my fingers, only to see that it was my own silky blonde hair I was holding in my hand. There was no doll at all. Stunned, I crawled from beneath the handmade quilts and tiptoed alone into the chilly living room where the coals in the fireplace had grown cold and gray. Maybe I had also dreamed that my parents had filled the stockings... and maybe... but no!

There was the little rubber doll with its staring, painted eyes. I couldn't get my stocking off the nail on the mantel, so I settled for a sticky-sweet thing called a coconut hut that was covered with dark brown chocolate that I didn't really like. It did nothing to stop the tears of disappointment from sliding down my cheeks. And that's how Mama found me... cold, forlorn and tearful on what was supposed to have been the happiest day of the year. Tenderly she scooped me, the last of her nine children, into her lap. Gently she rocked and crooned to me as though I were still a little baby. She called me her baby, too, but she said not to cry because William and Billie were coming that day from a faraway place called Houston, and they were bringing a real live baby girl for me to play with.

     William was my beloved brother Bill, who was almost grown when I was born, and I had not seen him for a whole year. I wanted to be happy that he was coming, but my heart was too heavy with it's crushing load of disappointment. I could hardly make myself eat any of the delicious country breakfast Mama and the older girls had set on the big round table. Her own homemade sausage came from the noisy pigs we'd been feeding. There was a huge platter of scrambled eggs from the hens Edna and I fed every day, with gravy, and biscuits buttered with what we'd churned ourselves in the big crockery churn. Homemade blackberry jam from berries we had picked in the summer! But I WASN'T pouting, as Edna accused. I was just heartbroken. Bill's shiny black Chevrolet pulled into the driveway back by the garage, and I dried my tears to greet him with his pretty wife and baby girl whose blonde hair and blue eyes matched my own. They were already in the house, hugging and kissing and unloading presents from the car when I got up from the table.

     Everyone had been handed a gift but me. It was more than I could bear. I slipped quietly to my bed and buried myself beneath the quilts to cry. Bill didn't understand my heartache, but he found me and told me to bring in one more package for him from the garage. I didn't want to go out in the snow from the warm bed but I'd do most anything for my brother Bill, so I pulled on the black rubber boots and my coat and trudged dutifully out to the garage. There was no gift-wrapped package in sight... only a bundle of white tissue paper with a hint of pink inside, lying on top of Mama's old steamer trunk. My heart leaped, but by now I was afraid to claim it for my own. Without opening the bundle I took it in the house and handed it to Bill. After all, it could have been for his own little girl. Bill tweaked my nose and laughed at me. "Well, silly! Don't you want it? What's wrong with you?" He lifted me in his big hands and swooped me up so high my head bumped the ceiling, then set me down with a firm thrust of the package into my arms.

Edna stood holding the sweater she'd received after boasting that she was too big for dolls, and watched my misery turn to unbelieving delight as the tissue paper fell from my hands to reveal the life-size baby doll with blue eyes that opened and closed! Her rosebud mouth had two "real" teeth, and there were dimples on the back of her delicate hands and on her knees. Blissfully, with trembling fingers, I felt for sure this time the silk of her dress embroidered with tiny flowers and edged with lace. The pink dress! The doll I'd prayed for and believed for so fervently ever since I had seen her in the big store in town!

Wouldn't any little girl scream with delight and dance around the room? I wanted to. I really did want to, and I know all the family expected it of me... but all I could do was hug her tightly to my heart and hide my face in her loveliness until I was told by the puzzled onlookers that my tears were making ugly circles on the pink silk dress.

Rebecca Bryant Hervey

Have a Blessed Christmas! I pray that God

answers your fervent prayers also, as He continues to do with mine and Reed's. We have a most wonderful promise in His Word...1st John 5:14 & 15...."Now this is the confidence we have in Him, that if we ask anything ACCORDING TO HIS WILL, He hears us. And if we know that He hears us, whatever we ask, we know that we have the petitions that we have asked of Him."

Can you think of any promise more exciting than that? Pray for what you need. Pray for your loved ones to come to Jesus! Pray for the peace of Jerusalem! Pray for the lost and homeless! Pray for God's will to be done on the earth. Commit everything to Him and listen to know that He hears you... then wait WITH JOY AND THANKSGIVING for your petitions to be granted!! What a wonderful God we have! We thank Him for His unspeakably wonderful gift... our Lord and Savior Jesus Christ... without Whom there would be no Christmas.

I love you with His precious love....**Becky**

"Candle"

Happy New Year!

As I sit here 'burning the midnight oil' so to speak... it's actually 2 a.m., I'm impressed of the Lord to write about candles. He likes to give me this private time at night when everyone is asleep and no phones will be ringing, to hear Him and do His bidding. His bidding for me is to write, and I love it! Thirty years or so ago I wrote a little poem, mostly to encourage myself. Things were really tough, and I had to struggle to be sure I meant anything to anyone... even to the Lord! Since then I've given the poem to lots of people, and even though it's sort of childish it touches hearts. Well, we're all God's children, aren't we?

A CANDLE IN GOD'S HAND

MY LIFE IS A LITTLE CANDLE... IT GIVES A
LITTLE LIGHT.
WHEN TROUBLES MAKE THE WORLD SEEM
DARK,
MY CANDLE SHINES SO BRIGHT!
WHAT MAKES MY CANDLE SHINE SO?
WHAT GIVES IT SUCH A GLOW?
IT'S THIS... I PLACED IT IN GOD'S HAND,
AND ALL THE WORLD SHOULD KNOW
THAT WHEN GOD HOLDS A CANDLE
HE MAKES IT SHINE SO STRONG
THAT EVEN IN THE DARKEST NIGHT
IT GIVES THE HEART A SONG.
I'LL NEVER HIDE MY CANDLE,

NOR TAKE IT FROM GOD'S HAND,
FOR IF I DID IT WOULD GROW DIM
NO MATTER WHERE I STAND.
AND IT WOULD SHED NO LIGHT FOR ME
OR OTHERS THAT I MEET.
'TWOULD BE A SHAME TO HAVE A FLAME
THAT GUIDED NO ONE'S FEET.

- Rebecca Bryant Hervey

We've moved upstairs from where we were, I think I mentioned that in the last letter. Now we have a room for our computers... the Lord has both of us writing pretty regularly, in some way or another. We're having so much fun decorating our new apartment "a la Pier 1 Imports". No, we didn't buy much of anything there... it's more expensive than we want to get into, but from garage sales, wholesale shops, re-sales, and our own stash of what I lovingly call "gewgaws" from boxes that were in storage...oh, yes, include WalMart and Target... we've put together something that expresses who we are personally.

We love candles, potpourri and incense! Natural woods. Hand-woven things. I have a few choice glass birds on an iron shelf by the window. Nothing expensive, but very satisfying to our eyes. You're welcome to come and visit, but it's a good idea to phone and make sure we'll be home because we just hop up and go at a moment's notice all the time!

As I placed candles here and there I realized that many of them have never been lit. And I also realized that some people like to keep candles that way. Nice, clean white wicks that will never be used. That's not for me. I want every candle in my house to give light and a sweet fragrance! I want the fragrance to reach out and welcome people into our home, and to bring comfort to the senses. And I fervently believe that's how God wants our lives to be. You and I are so privileged to be women!

We can radiate light and softness and colorfulness, and be candles in God's hand! Even if we're not writers, or speakers or singers or artists, we can each do something! A smile on your face will light up an entire room. I like to startle strangers with a smile, myself. A tired young mother in the grocery store or mall, weary from trying to shop with two or three youngsters to deal with... she needs a smile. And when I smile at her, she usually smiles back in spite of her mood. Maybe it makes her feel loved for that little instant, or encouraged.

We can also be very strong. Paul the apostle wrote of women as being weaker than men. I'm fully convinced that he meant physically, which doesn't bother me in the least. I don't mind letting guys do the heavy lifting and the 'macho' stuff! But God made women to be strong in other ways. Very strong and dependable. Check out Proverbs 31 again! Very strong! We have no need to be overbearing or controlling. We have God's ear when we pray for our husbands, because that is exactly what He wants us to do. Oh, sure, I express myself verbally when Reed and I have differences, and sometimes that's enough... but when I know he isn't hearing God OR me, I go into my closet and get alone with the Creator. Within a short time, Reed will mention to me that God has dealt with him about the very thing we'd argued about! It's far more effective than nagging or acting like a shrew, and lots more fun. He goes into his prayer closet and prays the same way for me when I get hard-headed about something, which doesn't happen real often, you understand, but now and then. :)

There are wonderful verses in Proverbs we should all keep in mind. It reminds those of us who are married to build up our relationship with our husbands, not tear them apart. Proverbs 12:4 is one. It says, "An excellent wife is the crown of her husband, but she who causes shame is like rottenness in his bones." And of course Prov. 14:1 "The wise woman builds her house, but the foolish pulls it down with her hands." A good man, as the song goes, is hard to find, so if you've got one who is good, honey, treat him right! Encourage him to be all that he can be, and never be considered rottenness in his bones. A man who's worth his salt will be appreciative and more loving. If not, pray for him!! Storm heaven on his behalf and don't give up unless God tells you to. Build your house and make it strong with God's help.

Be a candle in God's hand. I love the way it's written in the King James version in Proverbs 31:..."her candle goeth not out."

Let your sweet, strong, womanly light shine!

In His Sweet LOVE, **Becky**

"Watermelon"

Hi!

How's your year beginning? I understand that not everyone is standing in joyful celebration of everything that happens under your roof or in your family. Therefore I'm not going to start off like Pollyanna in the story and pretend everything is fine for everyone. I just want to say, "Hold on to God. He does all things well. Take your cares and prayers to Him and know that they are in good hands.. what greater hands can they be in than His, after all?"

When I awoke at 5:30 this morning thinking... ahhh, its Saturday and we can sleep late!... the Lord had a better idea. "Somebody out there needs to hear that small beginnings and hard times are not forever!" I lay there for a few minutes thinking of how, after so many years of waiting, planning, learning and getting so discouraged we thought we'd made the whole thing up ourselves... God spoke the word for things to begin to take place according to what He had shown us as far back as 1987. First a seed of an idea, then the sprouting of it in our minds and conversations... for Reed and I had not even met or heard of one another in 1987!

We met and became good friends in mid 1991. He visited my house almost daily just to use my word processor to type out ideas for a ministry God was showing him. We talked a lot! We also prayed a lot, and after a year we began to know that we would spend a LOT more time together as friends, but also as

husband and wife. We were married in October of 1992 in New Hope Baptist Church, Fouke, AR. The ceremony was performed by a good friend who knew Reed but was still a bit wary of him marrying... not just an older woman, but a C-c-c-c-c-Charismatic! Reed now heartily recommends both older AND Spirit-filled women. :) The basis of our marriage was, not physical or emotional passion, but a desire to serve God with every breath for the rest of our lives in the plans He had shown us. Now going on seven years we're almost like Siamese twins; where you see one you see the other, hating to be apart. God planted, He watered, He was patient with us and taught us through our mistakes as well as through His Word. Now our roots have deepened; we're sprouting and growing, and bearing fruit! It's time to tell you a story about a watermelon, now. It's called...
"WATERMELON WISDOM."

I was nineteen years old and pregnant with my second daughter. My precious mother had been buried only a few months earlier. My young Air Force husband had gone overseas, leaving me and our toddler Nancy Gayle with my dad on his little farm. Daddy had weathered many a storm, but that year was especially hard. Losing Mama was a crushing blow, and he spent far too much time in town at the pool hall and bar. This was not the Daddy I had known all my life! Sometimes he'd be gone for two or three days and I'd be scared out of my wits in the house alone at night. Hearing mice in the closet would send me racing for Daddy's old shotgun! It's funny now, but it wasn't then. I had led a very sheltered life up to that year and had never, ever been left alone at night.

It was also a year of drought. Although Daddy planted his crops early and they'd sprouted, the rains didn't come for over a month, and that just about spells the end for farming. Cornstalks were turning orange at the roots... a really bad sign, and the little watermelon vines were withering. I loved watermelon!! Maybe I couldn't do anything about the corn, but I WOULD help the melon vines! Daddy had been gone all day, and the vines looked worse than the day before. The well was not far from the north end of the garden, so I snaked the hose out there and soaked each and every vine it would reach.

By the next morning they indeed looked better, but when Daddy saw what I had done, he was upset! "You can't water a melon vine in a drought, Rebecca, and expect it to make good melons", he said sternly. He said that a melon worth its salt would send its roots down deeper into the ground to find moisture, along with nutrients from the soil and therefore its fruit would be sweeter, though maybe smaller. Seeing that I didn't really believe him, he assigned to me the first vine near the well, saying that I could water it all I wanted to as long as I didn't water it while the sun was hot because that would cook the vines and the whole thing would die.

I carefully tended that one vine all summer, watering it only in late evening after the ground around it had cooled from the heat of the day. It outshone Daddy's dark little vines so much I couldn't help looking smugly superior! My melon was at least twice as big as Daddy's, and a brighter, prettier green. Finally came the day when the little curl at the bloom end of the melon

31

dried up and fell off, and it was time to see just who had the better melon! Mine was first to be cut, and the green rind burst with a delicious "POP!" as the knife cut into it, revealing a gorgeous, if somewhat pale, edible part. I took a piece right from the heart, where a melon is richest. Hmmm? where was the sweetness? It was very juicy, but nearly tasteless! As Daddy cut one of his smaller-than-a basketball melons with its ugly dark rind it burst with the same delicious sound, but revealed rich, red melon-flesh! "Now taste this.", Daddy said, offering me a slice of his fruit that had struggled and made its own way without being pampered and artificially watered.

THERE was a watermelon! Rich and sweet, like the ones I'd tasted all my life from his crops, never knowing his secret! He didn't need to say "I told you so." I saw plainly what the lesson was. Later in life I would also come to know that helping something grow artificially is not always the best thing to do. A baby chick pipping its shell before hatching needs to work at getting out of that shell so it will develop strength for living after it's hatched. A butterfly struggling fiercely to free itself from a sticky cocoon MUST work at it and develop strength to fly, not to mention that if a person tears away the silky strands of the cocoon in trying to help the butterfly, he could rip holes in the delicate wings that must dry in the air and grow strong as they come forth little by little as God intended, ... or even tear them off! With a watermelon, as well as with a child, a marriage, or a ministry, we can and should cultivate the soil; making sure our plant has every opportunity to receive proper nutrients and a good place to grow. But we must also allow the object of our attention or affection to put down its own roots; find strength on its own rather than helping it develop a showy exterior with no sweet richness inside. Let it have its small beginning. Pray for it, nurture it, and watch it grow as God intended.

I love you, in His Sweet Love, **Becky**

"Feminist"

Hi, there!

It's been so good to hear from so many of you...
and some husbands, also, that God has blessed you
through these letters from my heart! That is my sole
purpose... to bless you and to please Him. Lately, as
most writers experience... a critical statement has been
made, just one, at that...that it sounds like I'm
"promoting feminism". Well... come on. I do make my
funny side remarks about why God created Eve. "It's
because Adam was just a rough draft", but that's only
to get a laugh, it's not a mean remark... and God did say
that it was not good for man to be alone, so He created a
help-mate for him. That means man was not sufficient
in himself to do everything God intended mankind to
do, right? Try having a baby, guys! :)

I'd never say that a woman could do all the things
God intended her to do without men being in the
picture, either! When I was in college 14 years ago, I
was seen as being pretty independent. Well, I had to
be! So I sure did look that way, but no one saw me at
night, asking the Lord for the mate He wanted me to
have, and crying out to Him in my loneliness and desire
to have a Godly husband. During this time of looking
self-assured and independent, a group of women asked
me to speak at a meeting where most of them were
militant, bitter, anti-men kind of gals. Well, laryngitis
came suddenly upon me, (Praise the Lord) or else I
might have been run out of their meeting, so I didn't go,
but I had written a poem which was picked up by a dear

old Christian professor and written into his curriculum!

Before writing it, I checked out the definition of the word "feminism" in the dictionary, and that's the definition I wrote about... "...advocating the granting of the same social, political, and economic rights to women as the ones granted to men." Now, right away, let me say that I don't touch politics! I don't discuss much about it because I don't really know the people who run for office, and I pray for God to place those in office that He ordains to be there. Is that a copout? Maybe, maybe not, knowing the power of prayer, but that's not what I'm writing about, either. And I wasn't writing the poem about letting women have their rights, either, I was actually chiding the militant women who named themselves "feminists" for the purpose of being independent of men. Maybe I was not wise to call myself a feminist, even though the Old Testament is full of examples of women called of God to fulfill things in all walks of life; but then again, the poem would not have attracted the attention of some who needed to be brought back to reality. I do believe God gave women an awesome position, and that is not to usurp authority but to use the authority and strengths that God gave to us. You see, the word "usurp" gets taken out of context also.. it means "forcefully taking the office, powers or rights of another", and I am certainly NOT saying that a woman should rule over her husband. It's just the opposite! My goal is to encourage women and men to see how the Bible tells us to relate to one another. It only really works harmoniously if BOTH go by the Book!

Would you like to read the poem I wrote? Do you think it encourages women to rebel, or just the opposite? I've printed it on a page by itself, and now that it's seven a.m. and I've been up three hours, I think I'll go back to bed for an hour or so!

Reed heard my letter and poem, and adds his thoughts, "Stop and think about it; every invention, every concept, every man who ever did anything, even the Savior, came through the womb of a woman... even the man who suggested that this writing is "feminist", came through the womb of a woman."

And now I'll close, thanking those of you who have contributed to printing and mailing expenses, and also those who have so lovingly and enthusiastically encouraged me with your letters and hugs!

I love you with the Sweet Love of Jesus! **Becky**

"Feminist" past Militance

You've heard me proclaim "I'm not militant."
well let me explain my phrase.
It's wanting some definition...
"militant" represents just one phase.

The word, to me, sounds warlike,
and I've already won the battle,
so why should I flaunt a uniform
or engage in bitter prattle?

A militant, wounded tigress,
reacting in panic and pain,
seeking only retaliation,
strikes wildly and makes no gain.

It's really not manhood in general
that I'm contending with.
It's foolish ideas we've all been taught
that propagate a myth.

Don't follow, like cows in a dairy herd,
the one with the loudest bell.
She could be reacting through bitterness
while missing the point as well!

We women who love the Bible believe
we're taught to revere our mate....
but the Maker revealed as He introduced Eve,
man alone couldn't carry the weight!

As woman, I am a nurturer;
a bearer of points of view
not mingled with tears of defensiveness
nor sot with romantic dew.

Here and there is a man with a sensible mind,
who knows woman's value and worth,
and doesn't exploit or belittle...
would God that they covered the earth!

So here on my soapbox of pen and ink,
I stand to expound in verse...
Be strong, be assured, and be WOMAN with joy!
Defensive and angry is worse.

"Pajaros"

"No Birds In The Nests Of Yesterday"

"No hay pajaros en los nidos de ayer". It's an old Spanish proverb, I'm told... pronounced something like "...no I pah-hah-ros en los needos day ah-yerr". When I first heard it, it delighted my senses. I know a little bit of Spanish, not enough to converse, but I think it is such a beautiful language! The wisdom in the saying, itself, is what stays with me. "There are no birds in the nests of yesterday." It's another way of saying, "Don't look back". Yesterday is gone. Tomorrow is yet to come. Today is where we live. Didn't Jesus say essentially the same thing in Matthew 6:28, ..."each day has enough troubles of its own"? There's no need to borrow troubles from the past. To do so would be to carry an unbearable load on our shoulders. The Lord has spent many years teaching me the truth of this, and I probably have yet to come to know the fullness of it, but its the main thing He seems to keep teaching me and drawing me to, time and again.

Lost opportunities. Lost loves. Stupid mistakes. Cruel mistreatment. Misunderstanding. Trying to live in "yesterdays" or to carry forward any bitterness and unforgiveness about things that happened in the past is like trying to find a fresh egg in an old bird nest. If you found any egg at all in an abandoned bird nest, chances are it would be either rotten, cracked, or completely dried up. Get the picture? And this is not about eggs, anyway, but live birds. There's no life in yesterday. We can give all our yesterdays to Jesus, because He knows what to do with them. He wipes away our sin, dries our tears, heals our heartaches. He even uses the "manure" of our past mistakes to fertilize our wisdom, because which of us has not learned some lesson from past mistakes? Me? I should grow some really great "wisdom roses" from the bushels of mistakes I've made, and learned from!

There's no need to be like those people who call themselves the "Penitentes". I saw some of them in New Mexico years ago... men walking mile after mile over the mountains, carrying saguaro cactus limbs, and with every step beating themselves on the back with the spiny cactus to atone for their sins. Surely they are very sincere people, but don't they know that Jesus has already accomplished that atonement? And have YOU done that lately? :) What's YOUR cactus that you beat yourself over the back with? Memories of past disobedience or foolishness? Even ignorance, where you might have sinned as a teenager, not really knowing how it displeased God and violated His commandments? You know, if Jesus had not suffered and died for us on the cross... if He had not carried our sins far away from us and washed us clean by His own blood, we might need to carry around a big cactus and punish ourselves. But no! Jesus took the punishment for us! All we have to do is realize that; receive His forgiveness, and live in thankfulness and obedience to Him! No one else on this earth has the power or authority to wash away our sins, no matter how hard they may punish themselves and no matter how much they may suffer.

And... no one else can give us power to overcome the things that made us do the foolish and ignorant things we've done. Or that we'll yet do! As long as we're in this flesh we're going to make mistakes. No one has ever lived a life free of mistakes except Jesus Himself...not even the disciples who loved Him and walked with Him those 3 1/2 years before His death on the cross. But we CAN live so close to Him that we do not WILFULLY or habitually sin. If we truly love Him, and follow Him as loving children, our actions will not be in disobedience to Him, wouldn't you agree?

Therefore.... if you are blood-bought, committed to righteousness, have confessed your sins before Him and repented, you can lay down the cactus! I have to remind Reed to do that now and then.... when he gets to regretting the past, or even things he's done in the recent past.... like rash decisions that wasted time or money. I bring out an old saying that my dad used, "Don't cry over spilt milk. " It means about the same as "No hay pajaros en los nidos de ayer". "What's done is done". "Let go and let God". Speaking of my dad... I've mentioned in other letters that he often quoted the Bible while raising his children. This same man harbored unforgiveness in his heart toward just about everyone who had ever offended him... up until just before his death at age 91. He had asked me to pray for him, because he could see that I knew the assurance of my salvation, and he did not.

Now, at that time I was 39 years old and had NEVER spoken back to my father in anger; but his illness, fear, and that ever-present unforgiving spirit caused him, one day, to step over the line and make me very angry. Finally, that same "Irish" that made HIM explode in rage at times backfired on him. In an outburst that shocked even myself I told him that the reason he didn't know the assurance of his salvation was because he was not saved and he was headed for hell!! I quoted

41

a Scripture verse or two to HIM... Matthew 6:14, 15..."For if you forgive men when they sin against you, your heavenly Father will also forgive you, But if you do not forgive men their sins, your Father will not forgive your sins."

Then, having silenced him with this, I called my niece to look after Granddad because I was afraid to stay home lest he bop me in the head with his cane as I slept! Neither did he want to stay home with me, so he had my niece put him on a plane to South Carolina, where my Baptist preacher brother-in-law led him on through to salvation... complete with forgiveness of all who'd offended him, I'm sure. Not long after that, Seth Henderson Bryant looked up from his hospital bed toward the ceiling. His face took on the most radiant smile imaginable, and he left that ravaged old body to spend eternity with his Lord and Savior, Jesus Christ.

I didn't see it happen, since I was not there, but at his funeral as he lay cold and lifeless... that radiant, indescribably beautiful smile that had never before graced his face, was still there! What a wonderful comfort to those of us who otherwise would have mourned his passing so much more. That heavenly, Heaven-bound smile! Did he see angels coming to carry him home? Did he see Mama welcoming him? Or did he see Jesus Himself saying, "Enter thou into the joy of the Lord"! Possibly all of the above. He had finally quit crying over spilt milk! He'd finally quit looking for birds in the nests of yesterday! He had let go... and let God! Praise Jesus for His sweet Love!

I love you very much, **Becky**

"Yellow"

Well, Good Morning... here at 3:50 a.m.!

The Lord has a wonderful sense of humor, doesn't He? He even got Reed up with me, because He knew that my mind would be like "bubble gum", as Reed puts it... all gummed up and without form. Ha! :) But at least I don't have to think much yet, because the word the Lord gave me to write about was "Yellow", which refers to a poem I wrote last summer in answer to one someone else wrote called "Purple". Purple was good.... it just wasn't "me", so I had to write my own, of course. Hope you get a giggle out of it. I'll print it on a page by itself, just in case you want to copy and share it with anyone.

I've always wondered what I'd do with the poems that pour out of me! Now I know... I can share some of them with you! My mind has always had a mind of it's own... so to speak. When I should have been doing homework in school days past, I'd be doodling pictures on the notebook paper, or making up poems or songs. Most of those poems and songs from schooldays are lost, but I still have a couple of drawings my proud brother Jim saved from when I was in 7th grade! He gave them back to me just a few years before he died... along with a set of ivory dominoes my dad had left at his house. I'd had no idea he had kept them for me, but it sure gave me a good warm feeling! Jim liked to hear me sing, too, and when I spent some months with him as he recovered from a stroke, he encouraged me to copyright the songs I've written so I could someday record them. Little did I know it would be 12 more years. Just goes to prove

43

that God completes what He begins in us... so take heart!

Some of the songs came to me as far back as 1969, 1971, and so on. I have sung them from time to time, mostly without accompaniment, but sometimes a talented soul would follow me at the piano as if he or she knew the song as well as I did! That is definitely a gift from God!

Anyway... where was I? Oh, yes! Songs. Well, at this ..ewwww, I nearly said "ripe old age"! At this, uh..... seasoned stage of life..:) {I really don't mind being 63... what scares me is the thought I'll turn 64 in July! Figure that!} At this seasoned stage of life, the Lord has finally revealed His plan to have the songs recorded and published. Not all of them, but most, plus one that a man named Geron Davis wrote that brings tears to the eye and stirs my soul ... called "In The Presence Of Jehovah". You've probably heard it by any number of recording artists. Anyway....thanks to the wonderful husband God gave me, and to the talented and patient musician /studio operator Bryan Jefferies, I've got an album recorded! Actually, it's my second album. The first was a cassette tape called "Sweet Gospel Jazz", where a few years ago we took some old favorites from the Baptist Hymnal, and Chip Bricker, another very talented musician/studio operator livened them up a little. Maybe we'll re-do that one some time, Lord willing and more aptly call it "Sweet Gospel Swing". We only published 100, and gave them away as 'seed'. The new one is on CD, and it's called "After All These Years". What else, huh? My loving husband did the insert for the CD case, and also for the cassette case. He's very talented and also very, very patient! Hopefully we can offer these for sale soon.

44

It's absolutely amazing to me how the Lord's plans are so much better than mine, yet it seems to take Him forever to accomplish some of them.:} It's actually to His glory, to keep me "on hold" all this time... and just when I decided that I might as well hang up and forget the things I could do, He turns on a switch and gets them going! I hope this also encourages YOU, when things look as though God has maybe forgotten you, or that what you can do doesn't matter. Don't get discouraged! He's just letting things proceed according to HIS timetable, which He wrote down for us before we were even born!

Who knows? You may have poems, songs, art, cooking or sewing talent or all sorts of things inside yourself that are screaming to be accomplished... well, maybe not screaming but just quietly nagging? Tell you what! Just commit all those things to Him who placed them in you, and tell Him to bring them to completion as He planned them, and meanwhile, work at them and file things away. Don't ever give up on your Creator! What He put into you was meant to glorify Him, and He wants you to work on it and perfect it so that when the time comes that He's ready.... your stuff will also be ready! So you're creative? So is our Creator! He definitely understands!

I just thrive on hearing how these letters bring joy and encouragement, and I keep all your notes and e-mails and letters on file, because they encourage me in return! Thanks so much!

I love you, with the sweetest love... of Jesus, our Creator and Lord, Becky (and now that it's 6 a.m., I'm going back to bed!).

WHEN I AM OLD

WHEN I'M AN OLD WOMAN I SHALL WEAR YELLOW WITH MY WHITE HAIR FLYING IN THE BREEZE OR IN A KNOT ATOP MY HEAD.

AND I SHALL SPEND MY PENSION ON HUMMING BIRD FEED AND PRETTY GLASS BIRDS, AND SAY I FORGOT TO BUY BUTTER.

I SHALL REST ON GRASSY LAWNS WHEN I AM TIRED, AND PICK CLOVER BLOSSOMS TO MAKE CROWNLETS FOR SOME CHILD AND TELL THEM, WHEN THEY'RE NAUGHTY, TO GO HOME.

TO MAKE UP FOR NAIVETE IN YOUTH, I SHALL SPEAK MY MIND THOUGH IT CONFLICT WITH SOME, FOR EVERYONE HAS OPINIONS PLENTEOUS AND VARIED AS BELLYBUTTONS. SOME ARE INNIES, SOME ARE OUTIES.

I SHALL STILL DANCE BAREFOOT IN THE RAIN AND GROW SO MANY FLOWERS MY FRIENDS WILL COME SIT AMONG THEM AND DRINK TEA.

I'LL PROBABLY WEAR MUU-MUUS TO HIDE THE SHAPE I'M IN, AND VOW TO EXERCISE..

AND THEN I'LL REALIZE I HAVEN'T HAD MY NAP SO I'LL RETIRE.

I'LL SNUGGLE UNDER QUILTS THAT I DON'T NEED, BECAUSE THEY'RE COZY, AND WAKE MYSELF UP SNORING!

YES, I'LL HOARD THINGS... IN BOXES AND BAGS AND DRAWERS AND SHELVES, FOR WHO CAN TELL WHEN SOMEBODY MIGHT BE IN NEED OF SUCH?

BUT FOR NOW I'LL TRY TO ACT WITH MORE DECORUM.

I'LL COMB MY GRAYING HAIR TO LOOK DISCREET, AND FIX MY DARLING'S BREAKFAST SOMETIME BEFORE NOON, AND WORK THE DAILY CROSSWORD AND READ THE COMIC STRIPS.

TOO LATE TO SET A GOOD EXAMPLE FOR MY CHILDREN.

IT'S THEIR PLACE NOW TO RAISE THEIR OWN DELIGHTFUL OR UNRULY BROOD, WHAT E'ER THE CASE...

AND I SHALL PUT SOME MAKEUP ON MY FACE AND FIND MY FRESHEST, BRIGHTEST YELLOW BLOUSE, AND LET THE WORLD OBSERVE THAT GROWING OLD BEGINS BEFORE YOU KNOW IT,

AND WEARING YELLOW IS A SIGN THAT I'M AWARE, AND I DON'T MIND, FOR GROWING OLD SHALL ONE DAY CEASE AND I WON'T BE HERE!

Rebecca Bryant Hervey, August 14, 1998

"My Prodigal"

Hi!

I knew it would come... this time in the middle of the night when the Lord would wake me up to write another letter to you! Instead of thinking, "Oh, Lord... I wanna sleep!", I get excited and sometimes downright worshipful when He gives me a subject to write about! This time I'm able to write in first-person terms what Luke wrote about in chapter 15, verse 23. "Let's have a feast and celebrate. For this son of mine was dead and is alive again; he was lost and is found."!!!! :) :) :)

I know first-hand how that father felt when his son came home! MY SON HAS COME HOME!, HALLELUJAH! Instead of killing the fatted calf we bought two cartfuls of groceries and supplies for housekeeping for the apartment my son Robbie and my grandson Daniel now share in this program the Lord has given us. I had dubbed the program "Honest Elbow Grease" in 1987 when the Lord laid it out for me... but the Lord has reminded me that He first spoke to me about such a program way back in 1971... and it was to be called "Turning". So, Turning, it is! :) Joyfully! For those of you who have just lately been added to my mailing list... this is a program that God has ordained and now sustains for giving all sorts of help to people who are tired of living according to the ways of the world and want to make a 180 degree turn to learn the Lord's ways and live by them, complete their education and develop into what God created them to be.

I had despaired of ever being able to operate such a program since it has taken so long... and I get older, and older, and older...:) But how old is God? He's the one doing this, not me. Not my dear husband Reed, who is so very much a part of what's happening. Not even a precious friend and co-worker, who came here one evening saying, "Well, here I am!, I don't know what for, but I'm here!", but she is definitely an integral part of what's happening. It's definitely not our own efforts to earn money to provide all that's needed here.... we haven't held a job with income in about 4 years now. We tried, even after the Lord spoke to us very firmly, saying, "I am your provider! I am your source!" Reed worked for the newspaper, and even took a paper route early in the mornings.. but the money he earned that month of December, 1995 all went for repairing the little Buick Skyhawk the Lord had so graciously given us cost-free. We call it the year "the Grinch stole Christmas", but we really know that it was our failure to trust God and not lean to our own understanding. Our 'Christmas Tree' that year was a potted plant.... a beautiful ivy I had trained to grow in the shape of a tree, decorated with 10 cents worth of blue glass baubles from a garage sale. We didn't feel sorry for ourselves, but we did sort of feel sad that we could not buy gifts for our family and grandchildren... but look what a gift God has provided that His children so casually and callously overlook! His own Son ... His only begotten Son!

The year after that was little better, and the following year was pathetic! Co-pastoring a little church in Stamps, Arkansas, we felt we were in a prison... broke, living in a converted 'fellowship hall' (with only one window) we had re-converted to an apartment. (The pastor and his wife had also lived there for a time). We were, as Reed so colorfully puts it, 'eatin' dirt'!

Sometimes we'd have nothing to eat but some dry tortillas, and I'd get sick from the dampness of those concrete walls and carpet that the rainwater seeped into. We prayed for income by our own hands... "LORD, give us a job! Anything!!! And a desperate call came from a person who hires people to deliver telephone books. Only Reed was hired, but I helped him. Our own little Buick was kaput by then, and we were driving his mother's ancient-but-usable Buick.

Cold winds turned to icy rain, and then to snow, as we drove to first one outlying city and then another, both windows open so we could throw those phone books in rural areas, small towns, and unbelievably out-of -the-way places! Not only did we freeze ourselves half to death and cause damage to the car, our arms were so injured from throwing those books day after day, sometimes for 8 hours a day that it took over a year for my right elbow to recover and not be in pain. But we ate!! Thank God we were able to buy food for ourselves and our sweet little poodle 'Lambchop"! I wore a black fake-fur coat I had made for myself in 1986, and it did keep me warm, but after over ten years of wash-and-wear it looked terrible! I reproached the Lord about it in my despair. "Lord, it just doesn't look very good for a daughter of the King to go around wearing the same homemade coat for ten years! I don't mean to be rebellious, but it looks like You could provide something better for me..." And that's when He said to me..."I didn't tell you to wear it!" He told me that if I would trust Him and get rid of that coat, He would give me all the coats I

51

wanted. (WHAT? Get rid of the only coat I owned?) But I knew it had been the Lord who said it to me, and He had also told me that Reed and I didn't need to live with a spirit of poverty. (WHAT? We'd been gladly suffering for His sake! We didn't realize that when He said He was our Provider that He really means what He says every time!)

To confirm what He told me, a dear lady in Bradley, AR phoned us to say she had cooked some fish and chicken and wanted us to come over and eat with her! Hallelujah! Fish and chicken was far better than dry tortillas! (I don't want to overlook the time a precious brother we'd never heard of, who lives in Louisiana, stopped by the little church 'fellowship hall' one rainy night, came in and visited with us, and obeyed the Lord by giving us a $20. bill, which was a great sacrifice for him at that time, God bless him!) But we put Lambchop in the car that evening this lady phoned, and went to feast on her fish and chicken, then afterwards visit in her living room, where she pointed out a black iron skillet on the floor, leaning against a chair! Few people we know decorate their living rooms with black iron skillets, so we asked her about it, and she told us that her daughter had brought it to her, saying that God had convicted her of living with a spirit of poverty and hoarding her extra iron skillet just in case something happened to her other one! Uh-oh.... there was our confirmation! Get rid of that coat I was holding onto for fear God would not provide another one!

So I hesitantly dropped the coat off the hanger onto the floor, thinking it would make a nice warm bed for Lambchop.... or that if worse came to worse I could always wash it again and wear it.:[Well, Lambchop tried it, but went back to sleeping on a plastic bag full of old clothes we had on the floor! Okay... if I freeze, I just freeze, I thought. So I put the coat out for the garbage men to pick up. Well, the snow melted... the weather warmed up, and I didn't even have any need for a heavy coat the rest of that season, but before long Reed was able to buy a new coat for me at JC Penney's, then my nephew Bob and his sweet wife Mary Ann (mostly Mary Ann..:) wrote to ask if I'd like a full-length 'faux mink' coat they had bought that had never been worn. It is gorgeous! At a garage sale we found an arctic jacket filled with down and lined with warm flannel that had also never been worn because it was too warm for the man who'd paid a LOT of money for it. We paid $5. for it. I never did need it because the weather was so warm, and finally this year I gave it to Gabriel, who had no warm jacket! He loves it. Then at another garage sale I found a cotton knit jacket that better suited my everyday needs, and I still wear it. It cost so little I don't even remember!

Needless to say, we have not worked at a paying job since then, but simply trusted and obeyed the Lord, who keeps us very busy and pays us well in the strangest way! No... we don't rob banks! :) Our only 'reportable' income besides what God has given us almost miraculously is a sometimes-life-saving $30. check from a precious friend who's been sending it monthly for about seven years or more! God bless her! Now God is blessing us by making the "Turning" program so alive that besides our own apartment, we can rent three others to house two young couples with a baby each, one of whom is a grandson I'd despaired of ever changing his errant ways, and my 'returned' son who has lived in despair and rebellion for 25 years, and another grandson, Daniel! 'Kill the fatted calf! We're celebrating!' Is it any accident that my eyes just lit on Luke 17:6, "Jesus replied, "If you have faith as small as a mustard seed, you can say to this mulberry tree, 'Be uprooted and planted in the sea', and it will obey you." (NIV) Jesus has already given YOU a measure of faith... start talking to that tree that's in your way!

I LOVE YOU WITH THAT SWEETEST LOVE
OF ALL, THE LOVE OF JESUS
CHRIST... THE KING! **Becky**

"Priority"

Good Morning to Youooooooo!

Uh-huh... it's 5 a.m. Do you know where your priorities are? That's a question the Lord is having me ask this week. Priorities. First and foremost things. Most important things.

I know, at this hour, one would probably say..."Yes! I need to be sleeping!" Well, I actually thought, when the Lord woke me up half an hour ago, that it was 5:30 then! I made a pot of coffee, turned the TV on and heard BeBe Winans worshipping the Lord in song. I seasoned and browned the little pot roast I bought yesterday and stuck it in the oven.... and as I sat down here to write what the Lord told me to... I looked at my clock! Oh, well! What's new? Praise Jesus!

Y'know... when we got home from Lift Group last night there was a message on our phone from one of the latest people to be put on our mailing list. The voice sounded offended, and she didn't give her name, only her mailing address. She said she had received two of my letters and didn't want to receive anymore, and wanted to be taken off my list. Okay. That's fine. I appreciate her letting us know, actually. We know that this letter is ministering to many of you, and that's wonderful! So.... I'm not everyone's cup of tea. I did the same thing to some TV evangelists who sent me tons of unwanted mail until I wrote and told them to save their postage because I didn't want their mail. I'll just say, briefly, that if any more of you would like your name removed from our list you're welcome to say so. Our aim is not to offend, but to encourage. We don't beg for money, we just want to be obedient to the Lord. I'd have to be nuts to wake myself up in the wee hours to write letters, and spend over $40. a week on postage alone, not to mention the cost of printing and processing the letters... unless... the Lord told me to do it. (By the way, if you submit someone's name and address for us to send them these letters, please inform them that you have done so, because some people don't like getting mail from a person they don't know. And we've had a couple of other phone calls from people with rude attitudes, wanting to know why we're sending letters to their mother, wife, or whoever! That makes us feel as if we've intruded where we shouldn't have.)

But back to priorities... In my opinion, one has to be nuts NOT to obey the Lord! He is our priority. Nothing is nearly as important in mine and Reed's life as doing what the Lord tells us to do... what He has placed us upon this earth to do. We don't do it for bragging rights, that's for sure, and if I seem to be bragging in some of these letters, it's not about us! It's about the things God is doing in the lives of formerly hopeless individuals ... and allowing Reed and myself to be a part of it! It's written in Lamentations 3:21-25 *"This I recall to my mind, therefore I have hope. It is of the Lord's mercies that we are not consumed, because His compassions fail not. They are new every morning: Great is Thy faithfulness. The Lord is my portion, saith my soul; therefore will I hope in Him."* Jesus is worthy of being the priority of every living soul upon this earth, don't you agree? We rob God of His place in all of creation if we don't place Him first. Some people take very lightly the words in Genesis 1;1 "In the beginning God"... and also that Jesus is the Alpha and the Omega... the beginning and the end. How can we place our own selves and concerns in front of His sovereignty? But lots of folks do. Even though in Malachi 3 it's written that man is cursed with a curse for robbing God...(v.9) and still , folks wonder why the devourer is eating up all their goods and blocking their blessings. Well! Can we give God leftovers.... (providing there's anything left) and still expect His blessings?

When we make Him our priority, He promises to rebuke the devourer for our sakes, and to open the windows of heaven and pour out such a blessing there won't be room enough to receive it! Hel-lo-o-o- do you know where your priorities are? Reed just put in his thoughts on this..."Life is actually a very simple formula... if you want God's blessings in your life, it's **'obedience to God equals promises fulfilled; and blessings.'** In Scripture it's written, "Seek ye first the Kingdom of God and His righteousness, and all these things shall be added unto you." Hmmmm ...could it be said that one who does not apply these truths to his or her life does not believe God? Now don't think for one minute that I'm going to give a plea for offerings at this point. That is MISSING the point altogether. We have a number of friends, relatives, and acquaintances who are struggling financially and in other ways... and I mean, drastically!..who are Spirit-filled Christians. They profess to love the Lord and they're usually in church at one place or another ... BUT they say they're unable to tithe. They say they just can not afford it. Well.... they've afforded just about anything else their hearts desired, even to putting it on credit payments with interest they can ill-afford, but they do manage to do that. We as friends and family, would like to see these people prospering and being blessed as God promises! Is there any way to open their eyes so they can see how to arrange their priorities? Hopefully some of these folks will see their condition in this letter and, rather than be offended because I seem to be pointing fingers, take it seriously and give God His rightful place in everything they have and in all they do.

Reed says...(having been there)... it was not until he got a revelation of the tithe and what God expects concerning it, that he began to tithe. He says he understands that it's very hard to remember that your main objective was to drain the swamp when you're up to your neck in alligators. That's some of his Lost Prairie Logic. :)   It may not be too clear to some who don't know Reed, but it boils down to priorities... and most people would think the first thing to do would be to fight the alligators, but he's saying that the alligators would not have multiplied if the swamp had been drained in the first place. Remember the priority.... the main objective.

And I say... it's 7:30 and I smell roast beef, and it's time to put vegetables in with it so it can finish cooking! Oops! I forgot to buy more potatoes! Well... I guess the potatoes weren't the main objective, the roast beef was. :)   Hey.. I hear the young folks downstairs, leaving happily for their morning college classes! What a beautiful noise! Thank God for His blessings! And I really thank those of you who write or call, and those who tuck a little something in to bless this ministry. You keep me encouraged as I obey God in encouraging you.

I love you with the love of the Lord,
and appreciate you! **Becky**

"Plastic"

Hi! How's it going with you?

I hate to admit, with all my "spirituality", that I'm snuffling and sneezing like just about everyone else. How long does this stuff last? It's more of a nuisance than a sickness, but I'll sure be glad to get rid of it! My nose is raw from blowing it!

But that isn't what I got up to write about.... I suddenly woke to the words, "instant potatoes". It immediately brought to mind the days when my daughter Gayle was a teenager who rebelled against the then-new potato flakes, which I loved, but she called "plastic". Anything not genuine at that time was, to her, "plastic". Well, they were real potatoes, but not to Gayle. She wanted hers peeled, boiled, mashed... all the usual stuff, or not at all. I sort of think God is like that about Christianity. What do you think? Yes, we're all washed in the blood of Jesus when we come to Him and repent of our sins, die to our old life and become alive in Him... but how many today really take their 'being saved' that far? It's like a dear Baptist brother said.. (who will recognize himself in this letter if he reads his wife's mail :). "Yes! I believe in once saved, always saved, IF one is really saved in the first place." But let's take the word "repent". Here's my old Funk and Wagnall's dictionary again. REPENT: 'to feel remorse or regret, as for something one has done or failed to do; be contrite.. to change one's mind concerning past action. To feel remorse or regret for (an action, sin, etc.)" And upon doing this, the repentant one must TURN from that past action or sin, right? Now, where am I going with this? Don't we commit sins all the time? Isn't a sin a sin? I'm not just talking about sins here that are crimes.

Of course those must be repented of and turned from. But aren't we being 'plastic' if we fail to LIVE according to God's precepts? If we constantly complain instead of give God praise? Murmur. That's what the Israelites did on the long trip from Egypt when the Lord had Moses bring them out of bondage. No matter that they were no longer slaves! They still wanted to go back and be slaves because it was too hard to endure and reach God's land of promise. Maybe because it's too hard on our human nature we go so far as to obey what our body wants rather than obey God's command to stay pure and holy. Are we "plastic" Christians?" Well, I believe we are told to count ourselves dead to sin and alive to God in Christ Jesus. But there's a responsibility here that Paul mentions.... **"Do not LET sin reign in your mortal body so that you obey it's evil desires."** "Do not OFFER the parts of your body to sin, as instruments of wickedness, but rather offer yourselves to God, as those who have been brought from death to life; and offer the parts of your body to HIM as instruments of righteousness. For sin shall not be your master, because you are not under law, but under grace."

There are sins that 'Christians' allow their bodies and minds to commit... thinking that grace will cover it... but what about this Scripture? "Don't you know that when you offer yourselves to someone to obey him as slaves, you ARE slaves to the one you obey?.. whether you are slaves to sin, which leads to death, or to obedience, which leads to righteousness?" (Romans 6 is where I'm reading.) Paul is speaking about whole-heartedly obeying the form of teaching to which you were entrusted. He is NOT talking about taking liberties with something called "being saved" without being obedient to the precepts of God. It worries me when people get 'saved' and baptized, and their lives don't change one bit. They're still seen doing the things they did before they got 'saved', still filling their minds with things the unsaved world enjoys rather than keeping it clean and filled with the things of God.

Are we to continue to live according to the old sinful nature, or according to the Spirit of God? "Those who live according to the sinful nature have their minds set on what that nature desires." Hel-lo!! "But those who live in accordance with the Spirit have their minds set on what the Spirit desires. The mind of the sinful man is death, but the mind controlled by the Spirit is life and peace; the sinful mind is hostile to God. It does not submit to God's law, nor can it do so. Those controlled by the sinful nature cannot please God." See this big 'IF' in the next verse? 'You, however, are controlled not by the sinful nature but by the Spirit, IF the Spirit of God lives in you. IF anyone does not have the Spirit of Christ, he does NOT belong to Christ.'

It bothers me, as I'm sure it bothers God, that churches today offer 'cheap grace'. Plastic salvation. "Just come and get saved and baptized. We'll put your name on our list and count you as one of the great number of people who are getting saved through our ministry!" How horrible if we don't carefully teach them and warn them about that sinful nature that will continue to plague them unless they are truly and sincerely re-born. How neglectful of our call if we just usher them into the fellowship of the church if no one carefully nurtures them in the Word of God and makes sure that they know what truly being born again is about. I'm talking about DYING to the old self and being born again in Jesus Christ.

Who's going to be responsible for these little 'plastic christians' when their old sin nature pulls them farther and farther away from the salvation they thought they had? WE are responsible if we teach them half-truths and allow them to believe they are safe, when all they've bought is a cheap 'fire-insurance policy' with nothing to back it up. There are young people we see every week at church, some of whom have been baptized two or three times in a year... who still have not grasped the meaning of dying to their sinful nature. They just come back and get 'dipped' again and again, trying to feel clean because of what they've done. 'Dipped' is not baptized! Baptism is symbolic of DYING to our old life and rising to NEW LIFE in Jesus. It's not a cure-all. I can't tell them all, Reed can't tell them all, you can't even tell all of them, but some of you may be able to reach some of them! Teach them the whole truth, before 'cheap grace' lets them run to destruction and death without ever really knowing Jesus as a bride knows her husband, submitting herself to him without reservation. With nothing but 'plastic salvation', Jesus will one day say to them, "Depart from me, I never knew you"... and then He may look at you and me, and say "WHY didn't you teach them?" Wow! I didn't know I was going to write a sermon, but it is something that has been on mine and Reed's hearts for many years. I'm glad the Lord got me out of bed to do it, because I'm just as responsible for speaking the truth as you are.

I love you In Jesus! **Becky**

"Round Table"

Well, Hello!

When you least expect it... here's another 'book' from Becky. The Lord didn't wake me in the middle of the night this time, he beckoned me to the computer right in the middle of my day to write about:

God's Round Table....
Full Obedience Brings Blessings

When I was a little girl...(that was a long, long time ago, but I still remember some things very clearly...:)) my family sat down to eat at an enormous round oak table. There was Daddy, and Mama; brothers David, William, Bob, Edward and Curtis... and sisters Mary, Sarah, and Edna. All these sat in those wonderful high-back chairs that you see imitations of these days, with a pretty pattern carved into the wood... but I sat on a very special 'highchair'. It wasn't a chair at all... it was a 20 gallon oil drum, painted bright red, with a soft cushion on top. I loved it. It was mine alone and I was very proud of being its occupant. It stood high among the chairs around the table.

I love round tables! Nobody gets pushed off the corner! If the table gets crowded, everyone just scoots a little closer together and sometimes there's barely elbow-room, but it's cozy that way... and easier to pass the biscuits or the peas, or whatever. We always asked for what we wanted very politely or else we didn't get whatever it was we wanted. "Peas, please", would bring the bowl directly to whoever asked. "Chicken, please". "Biscuits, please". And out of Mama's seemingly endless supply of biscuits, peas, chicken and mashed potatoes came everything we asked for until we had all we needed.. that is "IF" we sat politely, and "IF" we came to the table with clean hands and faces and combed hair.. other wise we got sent away from the table to do those things and come back more presentable. There was no backtalk or complaining at our table...and if anyone spoke needlessly, our father's command of "Listen..." stopped that immediately. We loved him, but we definitely 'feared' him.

The Bible tells us that God's supply is endless. See Genesis 8:22.. "As long as the earth endures, seedtime and harvest, cold and heat, summer and winter, day and night will never cease". As it goes around, it comes around. It also tells us that His table is round. Where? Try Matthew 16:24 for starters... and that is REALLY the starter if you want to feed at God's table. "Then Jesus said to His disciples, "IF anyone would come after Me, he must **deny** himself, and take up his cross and **follow** Me." *Well! What does that have to do with eating at God's table?* Let's go all the way back to Deuteronomy 28. First verse, **"If you fully obey the Lord your God and carefully follow all His commands I give you today, The Lord your God will set you high above all nations on the earth. All these blessings will come upon you and accompany you if you obey the Lord your God."** As your obedience goes around, God's blessings come around. Wow! Read those verses 3 through fourteen! Do you realize that your entire relationship with God... and whether you receive all the blessings He has for you.... or not.... hinges on choices you make? There are only TWO choices. There's the choice to obey God... and I mean FULLY, or there's the choice to disobey Him. How do you make the choice to **disobey** Him?... by not making the choice to **obey Him FULLY.** Clean and clear. Don't get the idea that disobeying Him is only when you openly rebel and turn your back on Him. *Not obeying him FULLY is the same as disobeying Him,* as King Saul found out to his sorrow in the book of 1 Samuel. Read v. 52 of chapter 14, and go on to ch. 15:1-3, and then verses 7-23. GOD WANTS **FULL OBEDIENCE...** Does your Bible say "FULLY" in Deuteronomy 28:14? Maybe it's the King James Version and just says "ALL"... well, its the same thing. "If you FULLY obey the Lord your God and carefully follow **ALL** His commands I give you today, the Lord your God will set you high above all the nations on earth. ALL these blessings will come upon you and accompany you **IF** you fully obey". And for the flip side... read verse 15. "HOWEVER.... if you do NOT obey the Lord your God and do not carefully follow all His commands and decrees I am giving you today, all these CURSES will come upon you and OVERTAKE YOU." *Is that scary, or what?*

God's not just whistlin' when He said "The fear of the Lord is the beginning of wisdom." **You haven't even BEGUN to have wisdom if you don't fear the Lord.** That means take Him at His WORD. Take Him seriously... ALL the way! Have a holy, awesome respect for Him and for all that He says.

"How can I know what He says?" READ his WORD! But I don't know where to start!" Here's my

67

suggestion. It's what I did when I was too unlearned and fearful to know my right foot from my left... I had a Bible with the words of Jesus in red. I read the red! There is an enormous storehouse of learning just in the 'red'. It's a wonderful place to start. If you want to know the proper way to live and relate to others... read Proverbs! If you need comfort and need to know that you're not alone... that someone else has felt the things you now feel... Read the Psalms and Isaiah! Just get all that under your belt and your life will be changed drastically!

Have you read the Ten Commandments and felt that all those things are a bunch of 'legalism' that you can't possibly obey? Jesus said that you will be obeying them if you honestly "Love the Lord your God with **ALL your mind, ALL your heart and with ALL your soul, and with ALL your strength." and if you love your neighbor as yourself**." "How in the world do I do that?" Just make up your mind to do it and ask Jesus to help you. You may say..."But I don't even love myself! How can I love my neighbor?" Well, Jesus didn't put that part first... He first said, "Love the Lord your God with all your heart, soul, mind and strength." (Deuteronomy 6:5) and verse 13 "Fear the Lord your God. Serve Him only." Once you get to loving God with all your heart, soul, mind and strength, you're going to realize that self-love is not the problem anyway. You're going to realize that HE is in YOU, and that YOU are in HIM, and that's what really matters... and then love your neighbor that same way... with God's love. In the old King James version, in 1 Corinthians 8:1.. the word is 'charity'. It says, "Charity edifieth". That means "Love builds up". Building up is the opposite of tearing down, now isn't it? It says..."**Charity** is patient and kind, it does not envy, nor boast, is not proud, nor rude; not self- seeking, not easily angered, and it keeps no record of wrongs. Charity does not delight in evil but rejoices in the truth. It always protects, always trusts, always hopes, and always perseveres." God is telling us to **be charitable** with one another, **accepting** of one another just as we are, and not to tear one another down. Charitable means overlooking faults. We DO overlook our OWN faults, don't we? We certainly are overlooking our own faults if we're trying to correct someone else's vision when we can't see clearly ourselves!

This opens up a whole can of worms! We get baptized in the Holy Spirit, and we speak in tongues and we think we're on top of just about everything! Well... if we're tearing down our neighbor instead of building him up, we can speak in tongues until we turn blue and it means **absolutely nothing!** It's right there in the Word... in 1 Corinthians 13:1. *And this is the cue for those who are like I used to be... * _"There! I told you this "tongues" business was not anything I need!"_ but you're wrong. You **need** this gift from God **to build one another up,** so that you can bypass your carnal mind when you pray, and when you praise the Lord Almighty, **because your carnal mind cannot think the thoughts of God nor be obedient to Him.** You also need this Holy Ghost language to build yourself up on your most holy faith, according to Jude 20.. "But ye, beloved, building up yourselves on your most holy faith, praying in the Holy Ghost, keep yourselves in the love of God, looking for the mercy of our Lord Jesus Christ unto eternal life."

You can't even fully ask God for what you need

because only He knows fully what your needs are, and if you don't allow His Spirit to pray through you in a language your carnal mind can't understand and EDIT... then you can't pray the will of God for your life. How about that? But you also have to be 'charitable' with your neighbors... don't tear them down simply because their ways are not your ways, or their language or color is not your language or color! Get real!

"Well, what if I can't fully obey Him... I've read all those things in the Bible and I try to live by them, but I don't know what He's saying to ME!" **Are you His sheep? Read John 10:27.. "My sheep listen to My voice;** I know them, and they follow Me." Now, this gets (as Reed likes to say) "Four foot deeper'n a well!) In the KJV the word is 'hear', but in the NIV it's 'listen'. The NIV has 'Americanized' the language so we understand it more as it was meant. Remember when you were in school, and you could 'hear' the teacher okay, but you weren't really 'listening', and therefore you didn't know your next day's assignment, or you couldn't pass the test? This signifies the difference between those that are His sheep and those who are not listening and obeying. Those who are obeying are following with all their heart, soul, mind and strength.

They come to His table and receive from Him in abundance because they meet the requirements for receiving. If we come to His table with dirty hands... or hearts... we'll get sent away from that table until we get the matter clean, our prayers won't reach past the ceiling. No need to ask for anything, because the disobedient have... consciously or unconsciously... asked for curses instead of blessings. What goes around the table comes around the table... obedience to His commands brings His blessings to our hands. 1 John 3:21.. "Dear friends, IF our hearts do not condemn us, we have confidence before God and receive from Him anything we ask, **because we obey His command**; to believe in the name of His Son Jesus Christ, and to love one another as He commanded us." and 1 John 5:14, 15, "This is the confidence we have in approaching God; that if we ask anything **according to His will**, he hears us. And if we know that He hears us, we know that we have what we asked of Him." **If we 'hear' Him as we should, *with obedience that proves* we hear... He hears us... and answers abundantly!**

I think I'd better end this letter here... it has already become a 'book', for which I'm pretty well known. That's why my husband designed the letterhead for me... "A Note Letter Book from Becky" because notes and letters usually became 'books'. I hope it has blessed you.

I love you in the precious love of Jesus,
Becky Hervey